TAKING CARE OF YOUR TEMPLE

Companion Journal

JULIE A. WARD-WEATHINGTON, BSN RN

This journal
belongs to:

____

Introduction

Welcome to the Temple Care Takers Companion Journal. This journal is designed to support and guide you on your journey toward holistic health, honoring and caring for the temple that is your body, mind, and spirit. Inspired by the principles outlined in the Temple Care Takers manual, this journal serves as a practical tool to encourage daily reflections, cultivate awareness, and help you stay committed to your health goals. Feel free to add any personal reflections, prayers, or affirmations as you journey through this process.

Remember, every step you take is meaningful and brings you closer to the vibrant health and spiritual alignment that God desires for you. Stay committed, lean into grace when challenges arise, and celebrate each victory along the way.

Know that you are not alone—the Holy Spirit and a community of fellow "Temple Care Takers" walk this path with you. Let's begin this journey together toward wholeness, healing, and honoring the temple that God has entrusted to you.

Pastor Julie

How to Use This Journal?

1.) Set Your Intentions: Begin your journal by reflecting on why you are taking this journey. Write down your goals, motivations, and what you hope to achieve through this process. Return to this page whenever you need to realign your focus.

2.) Daily Entries: Use the daily pages to record your thoughts, emotions, and experiences. Document your meals, physical activity, spiritual practices, and any reflections that arise throughout your day. This consistent documentation will help you track your progress and identify areas for growth.

3.) Reflect Weekly: At the end of each week, take time to reflect on your journey. Use the reflection prompts provided to assess how you're doing spiritually, emotionally, and physically. Be honest and compassionate with yourself.

4.) Set Monthly Goals: At the start of each month, write out specific goals related to your health, spiritual growth, and overall well-being. Break these goals down into actionable steps, and review your progress at the end of the month.

5.)Incorporate Prayer and Affirmations: Each week includes space for prayer and affirmations. Use this section to communicate with God, reaffirm your intentions, and speak life into your journey.

6.) Track Progress and Adjust: As you continue to use this journal, take note of what's working well and what challenges you are facing. Use these insights to adjust your plan, set new goals, and celebrate your wins.

Take Inventory

Start Date:

What is the current state of your health?

____

____

____

____

List any known physical problems.

____

____

____

____

In terms of your health, what do you want?

____

____

____

____

What do you have to do to achieve what you want?

____

____

____

____

What healthy living roadblocks might you encounter?

____

____

____

____

____

What excuses might you encounter?

____

____

____

____

____

What can you do to counter the roadblocks and excuses you noted above?

____

____

____

____

____

3-Day Food Log

Use this section to record what you eat, what you wanted to eat, and what you almost ate.

Breakfast

Lunch

Dinner

Snacks

Day 2

Day 3

Breakfast

Lunch

Dinner

Snacks

What emotions are you experiencing after incorporating lifestyle changes?

____

____

____

____

Any mild detox symptoms (headache, fatigue, etc.)?

____

____

____

____

Any changes in your energy levels?

____

____

____

____

Any cessation in physical problems you previously noted?

____

____

____

____

Health Goals

GOAL #1	GOAL #2	GOAL #3

STEPS TO ACHIEVE GOAL#1 • STEPS TO ACHIEVE GOAL#2 • STEPS TO ACHIEVE GOAL#3

GOAL ACHIEVED? Yes ☐ No ☐

GOAL ACHIEVED? Yes ☐ No ☐

GOAL ACHIEVED? Yes ☐ No ☐

NOTES:

Did you meet your goals?

____

____

____

____

What have you discovered about yourself?

____

____

____

____

Additional Notes/Comments

____

____

____

____

____

____

____

____

____

____

____

____

____

Module 1

Reflections/Taking Inventory

Use this page to answer prompts from
Taking Care of Your Temple.

Spirit:

____

____

____

____

____

Soul:

____

____

____

____

____

Body:

____

____

____

____

Goals _______________

| **Goal(s)** | **Actionable Steps** |

Body

| **Goal(s)** | **Actionable Steps** |

Spirit

| **Goal(s)** | **Actionable Steps** |

Soul

Confession Scripture

Prayer/Affirmations

Weekly Food Log

Reflections

Use this section to journal whatever the Holy Spirit is saying to you.

Did you meet your goals?

____

____

____

____

What have you discovered about yourself?

____

____

____

____

Additional Notes/Comments

____

____

____

____

____

____

____

____

____

____

____

Module 2

Use this page to answer prompts from
Taking Care of Your Temple.

Spirit:

Soul:

Body:

Goals _______________

Body

Goal(s)   **Actionable Steps**

Spirit

Goal(s)   **Actionable Steps**

Soul

Goal(s)   **Actionable Steps**

Confession Scripture

Prayer/Affirmations

Weekly Food Log

Use this section to record what you eat, what you wanted to eat,
and what you almost ate.

N

TUE

D

THU

I

SAT

UN

Reflections

Use this section to journal whatever the Holy Spirit is saying to you.

Did you meet your goals?

What have you discovered about yourself?

Additional Notes/Comments

Module 3

Rebuilding from the Inside Out

Use this page to answer prompts from
Taking Care of Your Temple.

Spirit:

____

____

____

____

____

Soul:

____

____

____

____

____

Body:

____

____

____

____

____

Goals ________________

	Goal(s)	Actionable Steps
Body		
Spirit		
Soul		

Confession Scripture

Prayer/Affirmations

Weekly Food Log

Use this section to record what you eat, what you wanted to eat, and what you almost ate.

MON

TU

WED

THU

FRI

S

SUN

Reflections

Use this section to journal whatever the Holy Spirit is saying to you.

Did you meet your goals?

What have you discovered about yourself?

Additional Notes/Comments

Module 4

Restoration

Use this page to answer prompts from
Taking Care of Your Temple.

Spirit:

____

____

____

____

____

Soul:

____

____

____

____

____

Body:

____

____

____

____

____

Goals ________________

Goal(s)   **Actionable Steps**

Goal(s)   **Actionable Steps**

Goal(s)   **Actionable Steps**

Confession Scripture

Prayer/Affirmations

Weekly Food Log

Use this section to record what you eat, what you wanted to eat, and what you almost ate.

Reflections

Use this section to journal whatever the Holy Spirit is saying to you.

Did you meet your goals?

____

____

____

____

What have you discovered about yourself?

____

____

____

____

Additional Notes/Comments

____

____

____

____

____

____

____

____

____

____

____

____

Module 5

Renovation

Use this page to answer prompts from
Taking Care of Your Temple.

Spirit:

____

____

____

____

____

Soul:

____

____

____

____

____

Body:

____

____

____

____

____

Goals _______________________

<table>
<tr><th>Body</th><td>Goal(s)</td><td>Actionable Steps</td></tr>
<tr><th>Spirit</th><td>Goal(s)</td><td>Actionable Steps</td></tr>
<tr><th>Soul</th><td>Goal(s)</td><td>Actionable Steps</td></tr>
</table>

Confession Scripture

Prayer/Affirmations

Weekly Food Log

MON

TU

WED

THU

FRI

S

SUN

Reflections

Use this section to journal whatever the Holy Spirit is saying to you.

Did you meet your goals?

What have you discovered about yourself?

Additional Notes/Comments

Module 6

Refreshing Reflection

Use this page to answer prompts from
Taking Care of Your Temple.

Spirit:

____

____

____

____

____

Soul:

____

____

____

____

____

Body:

____

____

____

____

Goals ________________

Body

Goal(s)

Actionable Steps

Spirit

Goal(s)

Actionable Steps

Soul

Goal(s)

Actionable Steps

Confession Scripture

Prayer/Affirmations

Weekly Food Log

*Use this section to record what you eat, what you wanted to eat,
and what you almost ate.*

TUE

THU

SAT

UN

Reflections

Use this section to journal whatever the Holy Spirit is saying to you.

Did you meet your goals?

What have you discovered about yourself?

Additional Notes/Comments

Module 7

Remaining

Use this page to answer prompts from
Taking Care of Your Temple.

Spirit:

____

____

____

____

____

Soul:

____

____

____

____

____

Body:

____

____

____

____

Body

Goal(s)

Actionable Steps

Spirit

Goal(s)

Actionable Steps

Soul

Goal(s)

Actionable Steps

Confession Scripture

Prayer/Affirmations

Weekly Food Log

MON

TU

WED

THU

FRI

S

SUN

Reflections

Use this section to journal whatever the Holy Spirit is saying to you.

Did you meet your goals?

____

____

____

____

What have you discovered about yourself?

____

____

____

____

Additional Notes/Comments

____

____

____

____

____

____

____

____

____

____

____

____

____

Additional Notes

Additional Notes

Additional Notes

Additional Notes

Additional Notes

Additional Notes

Additional Notes

Additional Notes

Additional Notes

Additional Notes

Additional Notes

Additional Notes

Additional Notes

Additional Notes

Additional Notes

Additional Notes

Additional Notes

www.ingramcontent.com/pod-product-compliance
Lightning Source LLC
Chambersburg PA
CBHW040159160726
48006CB00014B/1826